Passion PUNCH

to Success

Albert Garibaldi

Happy Publishing

Advance Praise

"Albert Garibaldi puts his Passion PUNCH into every area of his life — his family, his brilliant real estate career, and his stage presence. He is not willing to fail. I highly recommend you get his book, now!"

~ Mauricio Umansky, CEO, The Agency

"Albert Garibaldi is truly a unique human being. Albert is not just willing but also eager to sacrifice personal interest or glory for the team."

~ Gino Blefari, CEO, HSF Affiliates
(operates Berkshire Hathaway Home Services)

"I have watched Albert's success grow for two decades due to his clear understanding of two things… knowing WHY he does what he does and utilizing a commitment to PASSION in every one of his actions to accelerate his results. Thank you, Albert, for lighting up so many lives by sharing yourself through your books and presentations!"

~ John Thompson, COO, Intero Real Estate Services,
a Berkshire Hathaway Affiliate

"Albert Garibaldi is absolutely amazing! His life story will inspire you to live life to the fullest. Never underestimate your power within. He is testimony to how you can change your life to being confident, determined, passionate, and how to find that power that will drive you to riches and being the best that you can be."

~ Carol Zucchelli

"Albert Garibaldi is dynamic, engaging and emotionally involved with his audience. He is open, honest, direct and completely vulnerable, breaking down barriers and relaying more PASSION than any speaker I've heard. If you want your audience engaged and wanting more, look no further than Albert Garibaldi and his PASSION for success and helping others."

~David Bicknell

"Albert is a powerhouse business professional. He's bright, passionate, inspiring, and most of all he is selfless. He truly gives and brings tremendous value to everyone around him. Readers of his book can gain knowledge of what it's like to truly live your personal and professional life with the Passion PUNCH!"

~ Rishi Bakshi, Intero Real Estate Services,
a Berkshire Hathaway Affiliate

"Albert Garibaldi brings his passion to life in every keynote. He has abundant charisma, vibrant storytelling skills, and a teacher's heart!"

~ Sonia Medina-Ashby

"I've met many great speakers in the real estate industry, but you can't find a more natural speaker with a more effective, passionate delivery than Albert. The content is fantastic but the way he humanizes very tough topics makes his presentation a must for all sales professionals."

~ Robert Cruz

Dedication

I'm dedicating this book to my amazing kids, whom I love dearly: Dominic, Nicolino and Daniella. Before I started writing this book, I thought about what I wanted to leave behind for them once I'm no longer here. My success was built on being passionate about living life and truly being happy. My three kids struggle with challenges, just like we all do. I want them to understand that while everyone has challenges, passion trumps them all. It took me many months to finish this book. My kids were the "why" that inspired me to both write and bring it to completion. Life is too damn short, and now I've provided them a roadmap to find their passion. When they do, they will have a powerful PUNCH as they grow up and become amazing adults. They must understand that life is a gift and we're only on this planet for a short time. They only have one shot at this life, and I hope my book inspires them to not "goof" it up!

Table of Contents

Introduction

I failed the real estate exam three times.

People always ask me what drives me to get up every morning at 4:30 a.m. The answer is quite simple: I'm passionate about my health, family, friends, career, and life. Then they ask "WHY?"

It's the "WHY" that fuels the PASSION.

YOU HAVE ONE SHOT AT THIS LIFE. Don't f*** it up!

Life is a precious gift we're all given. We are only here for a short time. Make the most of it!

For me, I am always in touch with my why.

1

MY WHY:

1. Gives me the right to LIVE each day.
2. Leads me to be HEALTHY to serve my family, friends, and clients.
3. Gives me motivation to stay ALIVE to see my kids get married and walk my daughter down the aisle.
4. Makes sure I stay AWAY from seeing the doctor.
5. Guides me to be a ROLE MODEL to my kids and everyone else I surround myself with.

My goal in writing this book is for you to get inspired and take action. I built **The Passion PUNCH** to light a fire under you and inspire you to make the right choices to make you successful in whichever area of life you choose. What I'm about to share with you are the highlights of lessons that took me years to learn in a lifetime of ups, downs, and all points in between.

I overcame learning disabilities that caused me to doubt myself every step of the way. School was never easy for me, and every step I took carried obstacles with it. I learned from mentors, and I learned by working hard.

With all these handicaps, why am I experiencing success? Why does it seem so effortless? The answer lies within the title of this book: I truly found my passion. The more passionate I became, the more successful I became. It didn't take long for me to recognize the direct correlation between the two, and once I did, the sky was the limit. By harnessing my passion as the main driver of my success in all areas of life, I shot for the stars and never looked back.

This discovery was such a life-changing moment for me, that I literally sat down and brainstormed a list of all the words, expressions, and ideas that stemmed from the passion I have for my career, my personal life, and my health and fitness.

The more words that appeared on that list, the more I realized that ALL ROADS led back to passion. It drives everything for me, and it can do the same for you too.

My list eventually grew to about 65 words. They were all words that described and inspired me, and from this list I narrowed it down to 10. And from that top 10, I chose the five most powerful, impactful words that I knew could inspire myself and others to live with the same kind of passion that brought me to the dance in the first place, and that could keep me there for a lifetime.

Those five words built the Passion PUNCH.

The process of brainstorming the PUNCH involved taking a deep, hard look at myself to see what others could and couldn't see. I wanted to put to paper all the words that I believed held the key to a successful life, a healthy body, a harmonious family, and a successful business.

Now when anyone asks me why I get up at 4:30 a.m., my answer is simple. The PUNCH is what drives and motivates me, and by following the roadmap I'm about to lay out, you too can find your passion and experience similar or even greater results.

"How did you do it?"

This PUNCH to success is the core value system I follow in order to achieve success in my business, health, fitness, my spiritual life, and my personal life.

My wife DeAnna and I created a successful relationship that began 28 years ago, including 24 years of marital bliss. It requires discipline, time, and energy to build and maintain any successful relationship, and to cultivate a loving environment for our family.

In fitness, I challenge myself to keep reaching new heights, even as my body and mind grow older.

I proactively interviewed movers and shakers in my world about how they achieved success. Many of them extolled the virtues of the techniques and strategies they learned and utilized to become successful, but I also noticed something interesting. For all the success they were experiencing in business, they were nowhere near as successful in other areas of life. Why was that, I wondered?

Techniques or strategies by themselves are not universally effective. In the absence of passion, they are extremely limited and will not allow you to reach your full potential.

I chose to write this book because I wish to share the extra components that comprise the passion that was missing from their lives and that may be missing from yours. Not just techniques, strategies, or philosophies, but the actual passion. The passion, and the actions that follow from it, that made me successful in ALL areas of life.

If there's one single thing you take away from this book, it's to discover your passion. If you're not living with passion right here and now, then stop, read this book, and find it. Life is too short not to.

Even if you have learning disabilities, lack a college degree, or haven't achieved the success you think you deserve yet, this book is asking you to find your passion. If someone like me did it, then you can too.

When you know the steps and strategies, but don't have the passion to go along with it, everything takes longer to achieve. When a person begins to share his or her passion, success is amplified 10X and then 100X again.

I think a lot of people hide their passions. If that describes you, don't be shy. Don't just bring it out; FLAUNT it. Wear it on your sleeves. Shout it from the rooftops. Passion is CONTAGIOUS. Let the world know what you're passionate about. When you are fully passionate in your world, it is almost impossible to say No to you! People are willing to listen because they respect how happy and excited you are about what you're doing in your life.

Passion rules!

Albert Garibaldi
Top Producing Real Estate
Consultant & Advisor,
Motivational Speaker

CHAPTER 1

P is for Patience

The first rule of passion: passion goes hand in hand with patience.

Before you even begin to explore your passions, the first thing you need to inject yourself with is a healthy dose of patience. Patience is a non-negotiable prerequisite to any area of life you wish to achieve success in. The notion of an 'overnight success' is largely a myth; I challenge you to uncover any success story in which a great deal of patience wasn't displayed by those who worked hard for it.

The bottom line is that anything worth having is worth waiting and fighting for. What will determine your success is whether you are headed in the right direction, steadfast and determined with the energy and desire to make it to the top. Otherwise you will be spinning your wheels in an endless loop of misdirection, aimlessly wandering and wasting precious time. And unfortunately, the more time you waste going nowhere, the harder it is to practice the necessary patience you need to steer the ship.

Let's start with fitness, since that's how I choose to start every single day.

This does not mean that your days should mirror mine. The key to maintaining your patience is to find a schedule and routine that works for you. If you are religious or spiritual, you may choose to begin each day with meditation, prayer, yoga, or any other practice that brings you peace. If you're a parent, you might choose to drive your children to work before working on yourself.

Patience in Fitness

For me, I've found that early morning workouts work best for my lifestyle. It certainly helps that I'm a morning person, and by getting my exercise over with early in the day, I can focus on everything else without having it hang over my head. It's done, it's out of the way, and I don't have to worry about it.

At the risk of stating the obvious, getting into good shape does not happen overnight. It's for that very reason many people give up too soon, yet it's also the very same reason you absolutely must practice patience and consistency in this area.

The good news is that if you begin to do this, you will start seeing results. The positive results are usually enough to keep people motivated, so if you can get over that long, initial hurdle, it gets much easier from there.

I turned 50 this year, which means it's a constant battle to turn back the clock. While I'm not the star quarterback I was in school, I've still managed to sculpt my body into better shape than it was 10 years ago. This didn't happen by magic or with the snap of a finger; it took an incredible amount of patience and time in the gym.

There are a few actions you can take to make the process easier. First, **hold yourself accountable**. I share my progress with everyone on social media to hold myself accountable. By being held accountable, it almost guarantees I won't quit and risk embarrassing myself in front of my friends, family, and clients. More importantly, though, I don't want to look in the mirror and see the face of a quitter.

Second, **get help.** I have a personal trainer, which ensures I take the proper steps to get into top shape safely and efficiently, while minimizing injury risk. If a personal trainer isn't in your budget, I suggest joining a local gym or following a program you enjoy. Whether it's a book, DVD, YouTube, or a class you can join with friends, the key is to pick something you enjoy, perform it safely, and STICK TO IT. Only by seeing progress will you arm yourself with the patience you need to experience ultimate success.

Third, it's a smart idea to **switch up your workouts** and routines on a regular basis. As effective as the treadmill may be, for example, doing the same activity every day can get monotonous. Monotony leads to boredom, which leads to impatience. Instead, mix it up! Incorporate biking, swimming, hiking, dancing, outdoor activities, and then within those exercises, try to vary your routines. Your body responds when it's consistently challenged.

Lastly, I strongly suggest you **partner up with a friend** and exercise together. On any given day in the gym, I'll be joined by my 75-year-old mother, my teenage son, my wife, or my personal trainer. If possible, having a partner to share your journey with can make the whole process of staying fit far more enjoyable. And when you enjoy something, you're more likely to stick with it.

Patience in Relationships

Remember, we're after passion and success in ALL areas of your life. For me, I am deeply passionate about my relationship with my wife, DeAnna. We've been together for 28 years.

Perhaps nowhere will your patience be tested more harshly than in your relationship with your partner. No mystery here; relationships are a lot of work, and the turbulent roller coaster ride that comes with any long (and sometimes short) term relationship will test your patience like nothing you've ever experienced before. In a marriage, the level of patience required is magnified exponentially.

Patience and passion go hand in hand. As such, the key to a long-lasting relationship is the level of passion you and your partner have for each other. This is the tricky part, because many relationships begin with passion that slowly fades over time. Or maybe one partner has the passion, but the other doesn't.

In order to make your relationship last, both you and your partner **have to WANT it to last**. If that desire is there, everything else falls into place much more easily. It becomes easier to take the time to make it work, to overcome the inevitable challenges that will come, and to cruise pass the bumps in the road.

It's not a matter of WHEN you will face challenges, not if. The most important tool in your arsenal to overcome these challenges is **communication**. Both partners absolutely must commit to communicating often so that each side is heard, understood, and can offer solutions. If you'd like, solicit the help of friends, family, online communities, support groups, or trained professionals who specialize in couples' therapy. What will determine the outcome of your efforts is your level of commitment and passion you and your partner share for each other.

Almost everything is workable, and no matter how big of a challenge you may be facing, I can assure you that another couple has faced the same challenge before you, and subsequently conquered it. Have faith.

With that said, if you or your partner find that passion is lacking, and if all attempts to rekindle it have failed, there are no easy answers. If failure is the only option, do not despair. Just because it didn't work with one person doesn't mean it won't work with another. See it as an opportunity for both of you to rediscover that same passion with someone new.

If you're not in a relationship, and you desire to be in one, practice as much patience in FINDING a partner you're passionate about as you would if you were in a relationship with that partner. The extra time spent in finding someone who ignites you is well spent and will save you time you would've otherwise spent down the road with someone you rushed into prematurely.

The common ingredient here is patience, because that combined with passion will ensure a successful relationship. This goes for all relationships in your life, not just the romantic ones.

Patience in Your Career

For many of you, practicing patience in your career will be your most daunting task. The failure rate in business is exceedingly high, for example, causing most aspiring entrepreneurs to quit before they even had a chance. For someone trying to climb the corporate ladder, if success doesn't come quickly, it's very easy to give up and live a life of mediocrity. Don't let yourself become that person!

People look at my real estate success and often think it must've come easy. What they don't know is that I failed the real estate exam not once, not twice, but THREE times. I became best friends with the parking attendant at the testing center. Every time he saw me drive in, he'd tell me, "Albert, THIS time you're going to pass!"

It would've been extremely easy to give up

after even the first test failure, let alone the second, third, and fourth. Had I done so, I would not be selling homes today, would not be speaking on stage, and would definitely not have written this book.

You simply cannot quit or give up. In my profession, I see people try to make it in real estate and give up after only a short time. This is a huge mistake, and most of them have unknowingly robbed themselves of a promising, rewarding career they could've had if they had simply had more patience to succeed.

Patience is a requirement for success in ANY field, especially business and especially real estate.

How do you practice patience when it comes to your career? You already have! If you finished high school, you patiently waited 12 long years to get your diploma. If you finished college, you patiently waited 4 (and probably more) long years. If you finished graduate school, then you practiced the most patience of all. And in all cases, it was probably worth it for you.

Waiting patiently is not a standalone process.

Use that time to do whatever it takes to acquire the skills you need to succeed in your profession. Learn computer languages, software programs, project management techniques, or obtain certifications and degrees that will make you more valuable to your employer.

If you're in sales, use that time to constantly scout new clients and market yourself. If you own your own business, use every second of the day to market yourself while focusing on the delivering the best possible product or service.

Perhaps most importantly, take the time to **build solid RELATIONSHIPS** with people. If you nurture relationships built on trust, you will increase your odds of success dramatically.

In my own real estate career, success did not come quickly. Rather than give up, I spent several hours per day on the phone calling potential prospects. In addition to trying to land my first listing, I was also learning about real estate in general. If I landed clients, they would have questions on the escrow process, how to generate comps, how to stage a home for an open house, and of course, how to increase the asking price. Learning the ins and outs of real estate on its own took patience, let alone the task of drumming up business. I had to be prepared to hit the ground running.

No matter what field you are in, I propose that you embrace two ideas that undoubtedly took me to the next level: **mentorship and momentum**.

By partnering with a successful mentor to show you the ropes, you can drastically speed up your learning curve. By shadowing someone who is already where you want to be, you can learn firsthand things you will NOT learn in any textbook. Only through hands-on experience will you quickly acquire the skills you need to succeed. Think of it as free education. What's in it for your mentors? Free help! And by teaching you their craft, they will improve their own skill sets. (Just remember that when you succeed, return the favor and mentor others)

By building on momentum, you allow the hard work you did in the beginning to snowball forward and build upon itself. It's very difficult to stop an object in motion, especially when it's steamrolling downhill and gaining speed with every revolution. Once you land one sale, it becomes easier to land another. And then another. And then another and another. No matter your chosen craft, let momentum do much of the work for you as you begin to gain ground on achieving your goals.

Another critical thing to do is **be prompt**. I always answer my clients' texts and messages as soon as possible. Surveys have shown that people expect a response within one hour, so if you want to beat your competition, make it closer to 5 to 10 minutes. I might not be able to get on the phone right away, but I will answer and let them know when I can meet or answer their questions. Every second that goes by is a chance that person may ask someone else the same question. Be first, and you win. The next time that person has a question, he/she will come to you. Do that consistently, and you will win people over and become their go-to person. Fail to do this, and someone else will beat you to the punch.

By letting your passion drive you, you don't focus on the money. Lead with your passion,

I love working out with my son, Dominic

and the money will follow. Whatever your field, get into the business of building relationships, and your time, efforts, and goodwill will pay themselves forward in perpetuity. It sounds so simple, but building relationships is one of the core skills in any business or career, especially mine. If they trust you, they will want to do business with you.

Patience in Branding Yourself

Branding yourself is a long, arduous process. And, you guessed it, passion and patience are required in spades.

Building your own brand isn't just for business owners or salespeople. Even if you work in a cubicle for a large or small company, your success will shoot up if you learn to brand yourself. After all, we're ALL in the sales business. You're selling you, no matter which field you work in.

Fortunately, technology makes it easier than ever to brand yourself. Social media can make almost anyone a star, and your visibility and exposure are only limited to how far you want to take it. While it does take time to build your brand and establish a reputation, the seeds you plant now will grow into a bountiful harvest if you practice patience and display passion. Leads become referrals, which become converted sales, which then lead to more referrals and more sales. Momentum in action! Every minute you spend being patient is another minute momentum is being built.

The best way to make your brand stick is to **display an unparalleled level of passion**. Your competition may have more money, more experience, and more skills. They will NOT, however, have more passion. In a job interview, the candidate who displays the most passion, likability, and trust will almost always win over a candidate who has an Ivy League degree and superior skills. We are drawn to passionate people like bees to honey, and if you can get that burning desire across in your brand marketing, you will win.

Just remember to be patient.

Getting on the Phone

Another dirty little secret: I've never spent a dime advertising my business.

How is that possible? Perhaps because I was damn near broke when I started my real estate career. Instead, I picked up the phone and called people. I called friends, I called family, I called everyone I knew. If they didn't want my business, maybe they knew someone who did.

Everyone reading this has a phone, so it will cost you nothing extra. Pick up the phone, dial, and be patient and passionate about what you're asking for. Whether you're looking for sales leads, a better job, or clients to service, the telephone is your best friend. While an online advertisement may reach more people (and you should be doing that too, if it's free or low cost), nothing builds RELATIONSHIPS like a good old-fashioned telephone call. And as I've already established, solid, trusting relationships are the key to success in any area of life.

I will not lie: it takes a lot of phone calls to make this technique work. As such, your patience and ability to take rejection will be tested like never before. It's rare to find pictures of me without a Bluetooth attached to my ear. Call me a glorified telemarketer; I call it relationship building through the phone. And that takes time. Time, however, that's a well spent investment that will pay me dividends for years to come. I cannot begin to tell you how many homes I've sold that all stemmed for a simple cold call I made years ago. Does that time I spent seem like a waste now? You tell me.

By building relationships over time, I become the informational tool for my clients. People have a lot of questions about the overall real estate market, mortgage industry, interest rates, and everything else involved in buying and selling homes. My goal is to be the go-to person when they want information or to have their questions answered. When they do decide to buy or sell, they think of me because I was the one realtor who was patient with them. I answered all their questions and concerns regarding real estate and helped them along the way. I have past clients who call me out of the blue to thank me and express appreciation for how patient I was in answering all their questions. Most times they are questions that I've answered a million times before. I don't care! And neither do they. They just want information, and if I'm too impatient to give it to them, someone else will.

If they trust me, there's no need for them to interview anybody else, because I helped them along the way to build that trust and relationship, sometimes over a period of years.

Most people in your industry simply do not have any patience. In real estate, most agents want to find somebody who wants to buy and sell right now. Mentally, I prepare myself for the probability that many people don't want to sell right now. They want to time the market correctly and may not sell for another six months to a year. And that's fine, because with the patience I have, I know the business will come.

Perhaps the best example of this came in 2007, smack in the middle of the ashes of the burst housing bubble. While all the other realtors panicked over falling home values and houses going into foreclosure, I instead used that time to forge relationships with the banks. The result? I secured an REO account with a major bank, becoming one of their exclusive real estate agents for foreclosed homes. This resulted in my selling hundreds of homes while the other agents, who didn't take the time that I did to build any relationships, were forced out of the business.

By practicing patience and focusing on building important relationships, I turned a negative into a positive and cemented my brand and career at a time when others were quitting real estate altogether.

I will close the chapter with this: Patience takes time, but it's not a WASTE of time!

It takes patience to call people, build relationships, answer questions, wine and dine prospective clients, and even after all that, often get rejected in the end. Even if I win people over, they may not want to sell their home right away. When they do, though, I'll be the first person they call.

Here's the thing: patience and passion are both FREE. That alone puts you at a level playing field with your competition. If you can display more of either one, you WILL get what you're asking for. Passion trumps qualifications each and every time. This is your key to success, and the first step in winning in life is to practice PATIENCE in your passion punch to success.

Your 4-Step "Patience" Plan

Patience is difficult to maintain, especially when you're so anxious to be successful right now. The key is to recognize that the successful people you admire didn't experience success instantly either. Every single one of them expressed a tremendous deal of patience to get where they are.

To start with, **be patient with health and fitness**. Hold yourself accountable by sharing your progress with people and seek help if you need it. Whether it's a personal trainer or specific exercise program you want to follow, don't be afraid. To prevent boredom, switch up your workouts and, if possible, exercise with a friend. All these things will make the process much easier to follow through with as you wait for results.

Next, **be patient with your relationships**. Relationships are only successful for the long haul if both parties are passionate about WANTING it to last. To tackle any issues, communicate often and effectively, and seek help if necessary. It's better to end a cold relationship and start a passionate one, so if all else fails, it's not the end of the world. And if you're not in a relationship and desire to be in one, be patient about finding the right partner.

Third, **be patient in your career**. It will take time to grow and succeed, so use that time to learn skills and build solid relationships with people who will help you get to where you want to go. Find a mentor to learn more quickly, and use momentum to your advantage. Be prompt when responding to people, so that you're the first one to score wins that will advance your success.

Finally, **be patient in building your brand**. Display an unparalleled level of passion, and this will more than make up for any shortcomings you may have, and it will also distinguish you from your peers and competitors.

Practice all of the above and you will have the necessary **patience** required in your passion PUNCH to success!

*Wedding day with my beautiful bride DeAnna
in June, 1994*

CHAPTER 2

U is for
Unstoppable

Before my foray into real estate, I had hit rock bottom.

Living in the San Francisco Bay Area in the late 1990s, the economy was on fire thanks for a technology bubble that had yet to pop. Almost everyone had a great job and was making good money, and that included myself. It was a good time to be alive.

The loud pop came in 2001, and the bubble was no more. The expensive streets of San Francisco and San Jose were littered with well educated professionals who had been laid off, holding up signs begging for work. It was a sad sight, and I was not immune to this tech meltdown. My employer collapsed, sending me into a tailspin that gave me anxiety and panic attacks because the mortgage needed to get paid, and I had a wife and baby boy to support.

I had officially bottomed out. What to do?

Become *unstoppable*. What other choice was there? Doing nothing would've resulted in foreclosure and possibly homelessness. Failure wasn't an option. If I was to save my family and get back to the top, the only thing I could do was move upwards. Sinking further was impossible, because I was already at the bottom. I could either stay there and rot, or become unstoppable, swim to the top, and not let anything stand in my way.

It's easy to *say* you're unstoppable, but what does that really mean?

When you are unstoppable, you enter survival mode. If you were stranded on an island and facing starvation and death, you would do whatever it took to find food and water to stay alive. Nothing would stop you, because you'd literally have no other option. You would force yourself to drink muddy water, eat insects, or kill and roast any living creature just to get you through another day. It's a caveman mentality in which nothing on Earth is going to stop you from getting what you need.

What is it that you need? Make a list of your top three priorities, and list them in order. For me, there was no mistaking what the three most important things in my life are:

1. My health
2. My family and friends
3. My career

Allow me to clarify: my family and friends are the most important thing in my life, by far. They come first, before my career. However, the only way to best serve them is if my health allows me to. Without a fit, healthy self, my family and friends would have nothing. I don't take care of me in order to take care of ME. I take care of me in order to take care of THEM.

Once I'm taken care of, I can take care of those closest to me. And once I know those closest to me are taken care of, only then can I focus on my career.

How to Become Unstoppable

It goes without saying that passion fuels everything; that's what this whole book is about.

However, when it comes to becoming unstoppable, there are two separate components that are just as important: **energy** and **enthusiasm**.

Remember, we're in caveman mode here. In order to channel the unstoppable monster, you must adapt a SURVIVAL mindset.

For some of you, this won't be difficult. Depending on where you are in your life, you may already be in survival mode.

For the rest of you, if you're not starving, pretend that you are. Do whatever it takes to act as if you won't have food on the table for you or your family unless you become unstoppable.

Energy comes from survival. There are some days we all feel lethargic and want to throw the alarm clock across the room. We wake up against our will, forcing ourselves to get dressed and go to work. We might even skip the gym.

However, if you were stranded in the jungle, you wouldn't have time to yawn. You'd be amazed at the fight or flight response your body would take on, suddenly fully energized to run from the wild animals that would eat you for breakfast and hunting down your OWN breakfast.

Since most of us aren't running from lions and tigers, we must find other ways to create the energy required to become unstoppable. If you've done your homework and discovered your passion, you're more than halfway there. It's much easier to become energetic about something you enjoy and are passionate about.

Energy comes from what you put into your body, and what you put your body through. It is thus essential you nourish your body with healthy foods and proper exercise. This is not a book on nutrition, and I doubt most of you would need to read one anyway. It's not a matter of knowing what to eat or how to exercise, it's a matter of making it a priority.

Too tired to hit the gym? Go anyway. Once you start to warm up, you'll be far more energized than you would've been had you moped around all morning. Remember, if you sleep, you're someone else's breakfast.

And when you're done in the gym, feed your body with healthy, whole foods. You will unquestionably feel better and more energized, and combined with a more fit body, will provide you with the stamina and vitality you need to power through your day.

Health, fitness, passion, and adapting SURVIVAL mode will create the energy you need to become unstoppable.

Enthusiasm comes from energy, passion, and excitement.

Once you've harnessed your energy, enthusiasm isn't just easy, it's titillating. Energy takes a lot of work, and sometimes it isn't always pleasant. Enthusiasm, however, should always be fun.

It's fun because you've chosen something you're passionate about. It's exciting because your mind and body should come alive when you think and talk about it. Remember, passion *drives* everything else. If it's present, the rest falls into place rather easily. As the saying goes, when you love what you do, you never work a day in your life.

How do you know when you've found your passion? When you don't have to fake the enthusiasm. That's it.

Enthusiasm is a huge, integral part of passion. Your passion might be there, but without enthusiasm, it isn't *contagious*. That's what we're after. When your enthusiasm is contagious and infectious, others will gravitate towards you and want to align themselves with you. It's magnetic.

When I meet with clients, it's impossible to hide my energy and enthusiasm. They can instantly feel that I love what I do, and that makes it very hard to reject me. They want someone who will work for them with the same kind of zest they see when they meet me for the first time. They become infected by my glow and want to share on that journey with me. When people know that you love what you do, they want to be a part of it. That is the essence of what being unstoppable is.

We all know the feeling of when someone walks into the room and sucks the energy out of it. Nobody wants to be around that person. Instead, you want to be the person who walks into the room and energizes it. Everybody wants to be around that person. You want to create such a positive, radiant presence that when you leave the room, they miss you. If you can do this, success is guaranteed.

I know this works because I've done it countless times to convert leads into clients. Even if you're not in sales or real estate, becoming unstoppable will force management to take notice and want to promote you. You will find yourself drawing a small crowd wherever you go, simply because people like being around people who make them *feel* good. And you can't make others feel good unless YOU feel good.

I cannot tell you how many appointments I scheduled in which I won the listing simply because I was so enthusiastic. My energy made it very difficult for them to reject me. Most people only become positive after they've gotten the sale or listing. This is backwards thinking! You must do it the other way around. People feed off the energy of other people. Everybody wants to feel good. You must become their drug of choice. You want them addicted to you.

It's essential you understand the immeasurable benefits of having good energy and enthusiasm. When we communicate with other people, the communication breakdown is as follows: 7 percent is the actual words we speak; 38 percent is your tonality; and 55 percent is your body language.

What does this mean? By simply sounding and acting excited, passionate, and enthusiastic, you can get your point across no matter what you say. This represents a tremendous opportunity to win people over, regardless of your profession.

If you're interviewing for your dream job, you're far more likely to close the deal if you express more enthusiasm and energy than the other candidates who may be more qualified than you are. Re-read that sentence, it's critically important. You hold the keys to your own success within you.

That's how powerful passion is. It opens up a world of new opportunities you never thought were possible. Do you feel more energized and enthusiastic now?

You Only Have One Life

Every day you wake up above ground, breathing, and living, is a day you should be grateful for. You only get one chance at life, and you don't want to live it with any regrets. Every single day is a chance for you to make something new happen; don't let it go to waste.

Those words ring through my head as my alarm goes off at 4:30 in the morning and hit the gym. Those words help me become unstoppable.

We want our friends, family, and prospective clients to know that we are unstoppable and full of life. We've already discussed that energy and enthusiasm are the two main ways to become unstoppable. How else can we impart that onto those around us?

Do not discount your appearance and how you present yourself. In order to show others you are full of life, you must look and act like it. By being fit, healthy, and well groomed, there will be no denying your unstoppable zest for life. I always dress for success, because I know that if my clients see that I put that much effort into my body and myself,

then I will do the same for them. You are com-
peting with others who want the same job,
customers, clients, and goals that you want.
Your attitude will make the difference, and
much of that is visual.

A fit, healthy, well dressed, well-groomed
version of you will experience far more success than an unfit, unhealthy, slovenly version of you. It is your duty. You were blessed with life, and you owe it to yourself and
loved ones to make the most out of it for your
sake and for everyone else's sake.

It's easy to tell when someone else priori-
tizes business above health and fitness, or
above family and friends. By making health
and fitness your top priority, you can enjoy
your other priorities for a lifetime. The time
I spend with family and friends is enriched
when I feel good inside and out. By maintaining good health, I know I have a much high-
er chance of walking my daughter down the
aisle. And by being of sound body and mind,
I can be in top mental shape to build my career and business than I otherwise would be
able to.

While health and fitness were always on my

mind, it really hit me in my late 20s when my father passed away at the tender age of 52. My father always gave me an abundance of love, and now that I'm 50 years old myself, I want to take every action possible to live the life he wasn't able to. It's very difficult for me to write this book, speak on stage, win awards for real estate, and have three children knowing that my father isn't here to share it with me. He would've been so proud of me, and I want to live long enough to see my own children become successful and be proud of them. This is very important to me and a huge part of what drives me to get up early every morning and practice good health.

Unstoppable Energy = Effortless Success

The beauty of being unstoppable is that it automatically takes care of all the other elements that factor into your success. This frees up your body and mind to focus its energy elsewhere, thus requiring little to no effort on your part to worry about succeeding.

What do I mean? When you're unstoppable, you're attractive to those around you, and the law of attraction by definition brings more positivity into your life without even trying. This leaves more time for you to focus on and enjoy the other priorities in life, such as your family and friends.

Whereas sinking into a depressed state of despair leads to a vicious circle that compounds itself and makes it harder to dig out of, being unstoppable is the opposite. It leads to a POSITIVE vibe that attracts POSITIVE energy, and automatically builds momentum that forges ahead and makes it difficult to NOT be successful.

It all comes down to how badly you want it, and that again is fueled by passion, energy, enthusiasm, and survival. Those are your key words for this chapter; embrace them, understand them, and embody them. They're YOUR priorities, and they will drive you to obtain the happiness and success you want and deserve in life.

Unstoppable means consistency. This means that I stay on track even when things get rough. I always stick with my plans and projects, that's unstoppable for me. When you become unstoppable, you stand out. You will find also that you get less rejection. When you are unstoppable, you're more irresistible. When you have an unstoppable mindset, it's natural for people to join you, and want to be around you.

It's really about an unstoppable mindset. People that I surround myself with have a strong mindset. They are focused. When you are passionate, you are more productive, goal-oriented and you're excited to learn more. You focus on the positive things in life, not the negative things. You're energetic, happy, and fully engaged.

For me, because I am so happy, I'm eager to learn more, about people. I'm *genuinely* excited to hear more about what's going on with my clients. I'm very engaged, ask great questions, and give time to help them figure out what their goals are and find out what value I can bring to them. This comes easy because I love what I'm doing. This all adds up to an unstoppable mindset. I don't like to call myself a great salesperson; I'd rather think of myself as a great leader. To be a great leader, you must maintain a strong mindset. Passion and an UNSTOPPABLE mindset go hand in hand in your passion punch to success.

*My Uncle Rick, who severed his spinal cord in a horrible accident
that left him in a wheelchair. He is my best friend
and he inspires me every day.*

Your 5-Step "Unstoppable" Plan

Saying you're unstoppable is a lot easier than BEING unstoppable, so I devised a plan for you to get in that state of mind by taking action now.

First, **identify your top 3 priorities** and write them down. Mine are, in order: health and fitness, family and friends, and my career. Focus on these 3 things with laser-like precision. Without focus, you won't have anything to work towards.

Second, give yourself the **energy** required to become unstoppable. Energy doesn't come out of thin air, so you'll need to nourish your body with healthy foods and get enough sleep to recharge your batteries. Make sure you're passionate about what you're doing, or else it will feel forced. Enter survival mode and take on the caveman mentality in which failure is simply not an option, and that if you don't take action now, you'll become extinct.

Next, bring **enthusiasm** to the table. You do this by drawing on the energy, passion, and excitement you should already have by now. If you're having fun and enjoying what you're doing, enthusiasm is the easy part. It should be automatic.

Fourth, tell yourself **you only have one life**. Dress for success, paying attention to every little detail. Stay committed to health and fitness so you feel and look energetic, which will force people to take notice and advance yourself towards your goals.

Finally, **radiate positivity** and **remain consistent**. Positivity attracts more positivity in your life, just as negativity compounds itself too. It's much easier to stay positive when you're consistent with the actions you take to bring passion to your life. Once you start to see results from your efforts, being unstoppable becomes effortless because you know it works.

Practice everything here with vigor, and you'll become unstoppable in your passion PUNCH to success!

CHAPTER 3

N is for No Excuses

Passion knows no excuse.

The brain is a wonderful thing. It thinks, it processes, it remembers, it senses, and it's all wrapped up and protected inside that thick skulls of yours. While our hearts give us life, or brains enable us to live that life.

The brain, however, can play tricks on us. It's powerful enough to make us patient and unstoppable, yet destructive enough to sabotage our entire lives if we let it drown in negativity.

This chapter is all about re-training your brain for success.

What's Your Excuse?

Excuses are easy. They're a copout for when we do something wrong and don't want to really accept responsibility and take the blame for it. They also give us a reason to not do something we don't want to do, but that we know we *should* be doing.

Excuses are also adaptable. We can use them anywhere and everywhere. Too lazy to go to the gym? There are a number of excuses we can come up with, from not having enough time, to saying we feel tired, to claiming we're too busy with chores or errands, and to saying that we'll just go tomorrow instead.

And that's what makes excuses so abundant. They're so *easy* to come up with, and we can use them at any time, for any reason, to absolve ourselves of the blame and responsibility.

This is where your brain can work against you. By getting caught up in making excuses, you can drown yourself in them to the point where you never get anything done and never own up to your responsibilities. You think your brain is on your side, so it will always blame everything else instead of blaming yourself, because that would be too painful. Whether you're postponing a project, putting off chores, skipping workouts, ordering fast food instead of cooking something healthy at home, or delaying a task you don't really want to do, it's incredibly easy to instantly come up with dozens of reasons why you can't do it.

Your brain, optimistic little ball of gray matter that it is, also takes your side when it's convenient for you. It will make you think people will actually believe the excuses you put forth, and when those same people fake sympathy and understanding, your brain will actually make you think you believe them.

How to Re-Train Your Brain

In my day-to-day life, there are mundane tasks I don't necessarily want to do, yet I really *have* to. My brain plays games with me and creates excuses not to do them; it's human nature. If you find yourself doing this too, don't beat yourself up over it. Our brains are *wired* to do this, and we there's nothing we can do to stop it.

There IS, however, a lot we can do to reverse it.

For this step, you need to outsmart your own mind. Fortunately for you, our brains are very good at this.

For starters, you'll be pleased to know that it's normal for your mind to create excuses. It will send you messages that will enable the behavior you're after. This is why it's so incredibly easy to make a list of reasons why you can't do something you know you should be doing. If you don't want to take care of your relationship, or tend to your business, or take time for your health and fitness, your mind plays a lot of games.

Our brains respond to triggers. If you hear a song that you played at your wedding, for example, you will always think of your spouse whenever you hear that song. If you hear the repetitive "Turkey in the Straw" tune emanating from the ice cream truck strolling through your neighborhood, you will instantly think back to your childhood, playing in the street with your friends, rushing home to ask your parents for a few quarters and chase down the truck for a popsicle.

The trick to outsmarting your own mind is to use those triggers to your advantage. You do that by **flipping the switch**.

Every time your brain comes up with an excuse, *flip the switch*. Flipping the switch is an automatic response to negative triggers that come your way.

Every time you don't want to do something, your brain asks itself the question, "What are the reasons I shouldn't do this right now?" Instead, *flip the switch* and ask yourself a new question: "What are the reasons I SHOULD do this right now?"

Practice asking yourself this question every single time you're flooded with thoughts about a task you don't want to complete. The funny thing about our brains is that they <u>work for us</u>. If you ask it a question, it will find the answer. By *asking the right questions*, you can literally transform your life instantly. Asking the right questions is a skill it's imperative you acquire. It will make the difference between a passionate life and an unpassionate one.

Going back to our gym example, we already ran through some excuses for why you shouldn't go. This was easy, because we asked ourselves the wrong question ("Why shouldn't I go to the gym today?"). Instead, let's ask ourselves why we SHOULD go to the gym today.

Suddenly our brain is forced to search for the answer. We *flipped the switch*. What can you come up with? Why SHOULD you go to the gym today?

- If you don't, you will fall behind on your workouts and make it more difficult to catch up next time.
- You may fall into a pattern of skipping the gym and wipe out the progress you made and get out of shape again.
- You will feel energized after the first few minutes, and when you're done, you'll feel better about yourself and can attack the day with renewed focus.
- You will continue to make progress and come another inch closer to reaching your fitness goals.
- You can focus on other, more important and enjoyable tasks once your exercise is complete and out of the way.
- Your heart, muscles, and body will

become stronger, allowing you to pro-
long the life you're working so hard to
create for yourself.

- You will look better and feel better,
  which will in turn increase your odds
  of success in your career.
- By becoming fit and healthy, you can
  spend more quality time with your
  family and friends.

That is just a partial list that I came up with
off the top of my head. Keep going, and you
can come up with positive reasons why you
should do almost any task you don't feel like
doing. All because we asked the right questions.

By retraining your brain and flipping the
switch as an automatic response to negative
triggers, you lay the foundation for a life of
NO EXCUSES. And without any excuses, you
can accomplish almost anything.

Passion and Excuses

There is a reason I so badly want you to discover your passion, because once you do, it
changes everything.

When you have passion, your brain instinctively trains itself to NOT create excuses. And in the absence of excuses, you empower yourself to do all the things necessary to create the life you want for yourself. Nothing is standing in your way, and if anything creeps in, you have the power to crush it and keep on moving.

I've noticed this in my own life. Obviously there are facets of everyday life I'm not passionate about, such as doing the laundry, paying utility bills, ironing, vacuuming, and all the other usual suspects you can relate to. This lack of passion robs me of the strength I need to perform those tasks, and therefore it's easy to create excuses to avoid them.

By flipping the switch, I know that if I don't finish those tasks, I will drown in them and not have the time and energy I need to devote to my own passions: my health, my family and friends, and my career.

In my business, I'm passionate about serving people, helping them live their dream, and making it possible for them to buy their homes. Because I've discovered what drives me, I rarely come up with excuses to NOT go the extra mile and serve my clients.

I bring that same intensity into my relationship with my wife and kids. This enables me to serve them, make them happy, and provide the best possible life for them. Again, this demolishes any excuses that may seep into my brain, because passion trumps excuses each and every time. The same goes for my health and fitness. There are simply no excuses to not get up early and pulverize the weights in the gym, because I'm so passionate about living life to its fullest for as long as I possibly can.

Your New Normal

Starting right now, your new normal is that things WILL go wrong in your life. Life will throw curve balls at you, there will be bumps in the road, and there's nothing you can do to stop these obstacles from rearing their ugly heads.

The mistake people make is falling into despair whenever a challenge comes their way. They'll cry, curse, stomp on the ground, and wallow in pity just because something didn't go their way. Why? Because they falsely assumed everything was going to be perfect.

News flash: nothing is perfect. The sooner you realize this, the sooner you can arm yourself with the tools to overcome almost any obstacle.

Daily challenges, whether they present themselves in your career or personal life, must be incorporated into what you now recognize to be your new normal. By taking on this mindset, you will see daily challenges as a normal routine. If a day goes by where an obstacle *isn't* presented, that should *not* be normal.

There are two actions you must take as part of your battle plan to defeat the new normal: expect and embrace.

Remember, by reading this book you've already taken action to improve your life. When you strive to improve your life, you must take risks, tackle new responsibilities, and face new challenges that you wouldn't have if you had done nothing at all.

You took this action because you know the potential reward is worth it. As part of chasing the pot of gold at the end of the rainbow, you will encounter a deluge of stumbling blocks that may knock you down if you're not prepared to deal with them. In fact, even if you *are* prepared, they may still knock you down. And that's fine. What matters is that you get back up again.

When you **expect** hurdles in your path to the top, you are not shell-shocked when they occur. You may not know WHAT will happen to you tomorrow, but you will know SOMETHING will happen. By expecting it, you make it your new normal and can face it head-on.

When I have a challenge in real estate, the first thing I do is tell myself that this is normal. By doing this, I prevent myself from panicking. It's my own way of staying calm in any storm, and it displays the power and control I have when I *expect* to be sideswiped as a normal part of my daily routine.

Expecting challenges makes them okay, and I refrain from making the poor decisions that panicking usually lends itself to. Instead I can take a deep breath, step away from the situation, and rather than throw my phone across the room, I immediately dissect the problem and come up with a variety of solutions. Compare this to my competitors, who will blow a gasket and punch the wall five times by the time I've already brainstormed potential solutions and begun working on them.

This mindset goes hand in hand with not creating any excuses. Remember, if you're passionate about something, there are no excuses. There's no problem you're facing that someone before you hasn't already experienced and solved. There's no shortage of help at your immediate fingertips, whether it's an online forum where someone has already solved your problem, a YouTube video where someone can show you step by step how to fix something, or a telephone that can instantly reach someone who has your answers.

Be productive, useful, efficient, and practical instead of throwing inanimate objects against the wall. Own up to the responsibility, even if it's not your fault. *Expect* the unexpected.

Your next step is to **embrace** the unexpected.

That's right, I said to *embrace* the unexpected. Why would you want to embrace something that goes wrong and ruins your plans?

Because it's an opportunity to improve and grow. If you lick the problem this time, then next time you'll utterly destroy it with confidence, or better yet, prevent it from happening in the first place.

It may sound crazy, but sometimes when a deal doesn't go through or escrow is delayed with a client, I'll scream out of excitement in my office. My wife will often hear me and wonder what the good news is. "There IS no good news," I'll tell her. "It's AWFUL news! Yeah!!!"

This erratic response is how I've re-trained my brain to react to problems. I've already come to *expect* things like this to happen, so I don't have to go through the painful process of pounding the desk, asking 'why me?' and drowning myself in a sea of negative, destructive thoughts. I've already done that once for a lifetime of future problems! So when I get that phone call telling me awful news, I *embrace* it and get excited.

I embrace it because I know the possibilities can be even greater than the original outcome. Perhaps one dead deal can lead to another, more lucrative deal. Perhaps a buyer backing out of a home purchase will end up buying an even better home. Whatever the case, I will learn from it, grow from it, and be better for it so that NEXT time it happens, I will know what to do.

Have you ever been through a painful divorce or breakup? The first time you go through it, it feels like your world is falling apart. You let out your emotions, you grieve, and you get over it. And if it happens again, you know how to respond. If your friends go through it, you're better equipped to help them. You might even come to expect it, thus softening the blow.

My point is, by *embracing* problems, you can attack them with energy, vigor, and enthusiasm. You WON'T attack them with endless excuses that do nothing but pile up and suffocate you. When you live with passion, you can embrace almost any obstacle that comes your way.

Your 3-Step "No Excuses" Plan

Making excuses is ridiculously easy. Eliminating them is not so simple, so I devised a

3-step plan to help you pave the way for your own success without letting excuses get in your way:

First, re-train your brain by **flipping the switch**. Every time an excuse floats your way, turn the tables on it. Instead of asking yourself why you shouldn't do something, ask yourself why you *should*. You can even take it a step further and ask yourself what will happen if you *don't* complete the task at hand. Ask yourselves the right questions, and your brain will find the best answers.

Second, as part of your new normal, **expect** problems, obstacles, and challenges to come your way. You will wake up each day not knowing which fire you'll have to put out, but you will know to expect the fire. By bracing yourself for what may come, you will not be blindsided.

Lastly, **embrace** the bumps in the road. Rather than shouting expletives, shout "Yeah!" View each difficulty as an opportunity to learn, grow, and solve a new problem so that you'll crush it next time. Success comes first from failure, and we learn from mistakes and mishaps. By embracing this concept, you'll literally never have a problem again, because what you used to see as problems are now opportunities for improvement.

Don't let anything stop you, especially your brain. It's the most powerful organ in your body aside from your heart, and letting it outsmart you may threaten your journey to the top. Instead, use it to your advantage, and you will be left with no excuses in your passion PUNCH to success!

My mother often joins me in the gym, up and early

CHAPTER 4

C is for Courage

It takes courage to be passionate.

My grandmother did my homework. And she got a better grade than I would've.

In 1982, I was an insecure, pimply faced teenager who struggled with school. It was not for lack of effort, as I tried hard yet couldn't seem to follow the teachers' lectures as well as the other kids could. I began to think something was wrong with me, and my confidence fell to a new low with each failing grade I received on my exams and homework assignments.

Since I excelled at sports, my grades became even more important. My football coach begged and pleaded with the teachers, saying, "Albert is our star quarterback. Can you please pass him with a C-minus so that he can keep playing for us and not flunk out?"

It got so bad that I had to ask my 68-year-old grandmother to finish my book report for me. She read the book herself, wrote it up herself, and I put my name on it. My intentions were pure; I wasn't doing it to be lazy or cheat the system. I did it because I lacked the *courage* to admit that I couldn't.

The shame I felt when I handed in my grandmother's book report made me finally take action. I remember having to repeat the 2nd grade, and didn't want to do that again and fall further behind. With tears in my eyes, I asked my parents for help. I was fortunate to have been blessed with two loving parents, and without hesitation they sought professional help and had me tested to assess my mental aptitude.

The results were a huge relief for me, reading like a laundry list of words I had never heard before: Auditory Processing Disorder, Dyslexia, Language Processing Disorder, and ADHD.

While school never got easier for me, at least my learning disabilities boosted my confidence. No longer did I feel like the dumb jock in class. As the doctors told me, it's not that I couldn't learn, it's that I was wired differently than the other kids. Thank goodness I had the courage to admit my shortcomings and tell my parents, or else I wouldn't be writing this book.

What is Courage?

When we're kids, we first learn about courage by watching the Cowardly Lion in the *Wizard of Oz*. Courage is the only reason I'm successful in real estate and can stand in front of sold out crowds delivering my Passion Punch speeches. If you had told me in 1982 that one day I'd be on stage, inspiring and motivating people to discover their passions, I'd have thought you were from outer space. Only smart kids could do that, and I had convinced myself that I was an airhead no matter how much I studied.

Courage is a major component of success and works in tandem with everything else it takes to be passionate. If you have patience (P), if you become unstoppable (U), and if you give no excuses (N), then you certainly have what it takes to drink a healthy dose of courage (C).

You're often going to feel scared or timid to do some of the things this book is asking you to do. When I meet other realtors or people who have seen me speak, I will ask them what their passion punch looks like. Often they'll seem too weak, shy, embarrassed, or afraid to tell me with conviction. The only way to overcome those feelings is to stand up to them with courage. Without it, I'd still be in the back of the class, repeating the 12th grade at age 50, world famous as the America's oldest high school Senior.

Courage means taking the bull by the horns, facing your fears, and being brave enough to look them directly in the eye without backing down. Truth be told, you don't even have to be Godzilla. If you're afraid of public speaking, for example, and you simply sign up for Toastmasters, you've already taken a courageous step towards self-improvement. By taking that small baby step, you're well on your way to conquering your fear. Even starting small can reap huge rewards later on.

Remember, it took many, many years before I experienced major success in real estate. It all started with a tiny sip of courage before I was gulping it down by the gallon.

How to Acquire Courage

It's easy for me to tell you to *have* courage, yet without a tangible action plan, it won't mean much. There are actionable steps you can take today to help acquire the courage you will absolutely need to find and deliver your passion punch to success.

I have good news and bad news. The bad news is that the first step is the hardest, and it may scare you off before you even get started. The good news is that once you complete that first step, the rest becomes infinitely easier.

The #1 most important thing you must do right now is **get uncomfortable**. What do I mean? Identify your comfort zone, and get out of it now.

Do things that make you feel uncomfortable. If you want to succeed at anything in life, make yourself uncomfortable. Challenge yourself and do things that *terrify* you. By doing this consistently, you'll grow as a human being and create opportunities for yourself that you never thought were possible.

To my previous example, joining Toastmasters is a great way to exit your comfort zone and do something you're deathly afraid of (public speaking). Want to learn to think or speak on the fly? Take an improv class. Are you new in town and want to meet new people? Take salsa dance lessons with complete strangers. Are you eyeing a new job that requires you to travel to China? Sign up for Chinese language classes. Are you in the service business and not getting results with social media? Try marketing yourself by giving a free seminar, starting a podcast, or going to conventions and networking.

How do you know you've left your comfort zone? When you experience that feeling in your stomach that makes you afraid. When you feel fear, your discomfort zone is here.

Second, **prepare yourself**. Fear is based on the unknown. If you do your homework and prepare yourself for whatever it is you're afraid of, you'll know more and have a better idea of what to expect.

Back to our public speaking example, it's easy to go online and find a plethora of tips and techniques to help you become a better speaker. Write out your speech, practice it, and even deliver it in front of a few close friends or family members. Go to an empty auditorium and walk around when nobody is there, familiarizing yourself with your new surroundings. Become *numb* to what it is you fear, so that it no longer has a stranglehold on you. You get the picture.

Do a dry run. Speak in front of the mirror, record yourself, and be brutally honest. Embrace the unknown. Remember how scared you were when you got behind the wheel for the first time? Thousands of cars on the road, all roaming aimlessly and ready to crash into you headon. You had no experience changing lanes, parallel parking, or making a U-turn. Now you never even give it a second thought. As an infant, the thought of walking seemed like a daunting task, so you learned to crawl first. Then you wobbled your way across the playpen, falling down each time. A year later, you were running back and forth. This is how you master ANY new skill.

Finally, **bring a friend**. And if bringing a friend isn't possible (like starting a new career in real estate, for example), then find a **mentor**. Having someone there to either show you the ropes, or share in your learning experience, makes the process fun, humble, and far less stressful. Mentors can teach you to avoid certain mistakes and give you tips and tricks to master whatever it is you're trying. Friends make a great support system, and will give you some degree of familiarity in a sea of unknowns.

Courage in Action

Let's run through an example from my own life:

As I mentioned in the Chapter 2, my career completely bottomed out in 2001 following the collapse of the dotcom bubble. Suddenly out of work with a mortgage to pay and family to support, I completely stepped *out of my comfort zone* and chose an entirely new career I had zero experience in: real estate.

Talk about being uncomfortable, not only was

this industry all new to me, I was also stressing out because of the financial hardship I had put my family in. As any newly licensed realtor knows, there's no steady paycheck in real estate. Until you get your first listing, sell it, and escrow finally closes, you need some other means to feed yourself and your family. As my wife babysat to bring in extra money, I was an anxious, nervous wreck trying to learn a complicated new "job" that wasn't paying me a dime.

To make matters worse, my childhood came back to haunt me when it was time to take the real estate license exam. My learning disabilities never went away; they had just been masked by being out of school for 15 years and not having to take any tests since then. As you read earlier, and as you may have heard me confess in my speeches, it took me FIVE TRIES to finally pass the exam. And I only did so by enlisting the help of a tutor.

Next, I *prepared myself*. I became a voracious consumer of any knowledge and information I could find on the real estate industry. The good news was that I had solid experience as a successful salesperson, so I could focus on the inner workings of the escrow process and how to set asking prices instead of the much more difficult task of learning how to sell.

Still, it was all new to me. My only exposure to real estate was buying and selling my own home; a home I was going to lose unless I forced myself to become successful in this new venture.

To help speed up the learning curve, I befriended and *aligned myself* with a mentor who was already successfully selling homes. He took me under his wing and taught me everything there was to know, a luxury that almost every new real estate agent doesn't have because they don't take the time to find someone to help them. And it worked both ways; my mentor benefitted from my own success, which motivated him to teach me.

I cannot over emphasize how helpful it was to have someone show me the journey, taking me along on open houses, stepping me through escrow, giving me ideas on how to find prospects, and buying me tacos for lunch because I couldn't afford them. In fact, his help was so critical in my initial success and orientation that it's the primary reason I try to give back as much as possible today. It's why I wrote this book, it's why I go on speaking tours, and it's why I take whatever time I can to mentor others as well.

The example I outlined above for you is the very essence of <u>courage</u> and how to acquire it and utilize it to your advantage. Of course, none of this is possible without first finding your passion, and at this point that goes without saying. For without passion, you may never find the necessary courage to conquer your demons.

The Courage to CONNECT

Let's say you've exited your comfort zone, prepared yourself, and found a good friend or mentor to help give you courage. Congratulations, you're halfway there.

That's right, despite all you did to gain the courage you need to succeed, it is STILL not enough. If you want to be successful in life, you need to connect with people.

What does connection have to do with courage? Everything. Without courage, you cannot connect. And without a connection, your courage will only get you halfway where you want to go.

Multiple studies have shown that the number one quality people seek in a real estate professional is trust. Logic says that this would also hold true for other professions, and even in your personal life. Friendships and relationships, for example, are built on trust. Job candidates are hired based on trust. We vote for people we trust, and those same political leaders work to build relationships with other world leaders based on trust.

How do you earn trust? You get people to like you. And you've only got seconds to do it. If they like you, they trust you. And you get people to like you by building a connection with them.

I pride myself on the Intero Value award I won in 2009. However, if real estate gave out awards for connecting, I'd win that award too, each and every year.

What do I mean?

For me to connect with people and get them to like me, I have to match their personality type. Studies have consistently shown for years that we are drawn to people who talk, walk, act, and think like we do. Our body language, vocal tonality, speed of speech, and other personality traits can collectively attract or repel certain kinds of people.

It's the same reason social butterflies are attracted to other social people. Shy, introverted people are attracted to other shy, introverted people. There are volumes of books written on personality matching, and there are even job searching experts out there who say this is the #1 technique to use when interviewing for a job. To connect with people immediately, match their energy and personality as much as possible.

Whenever I meet with prospective clients for the first time, I immediately try to determine which personality type they are. Depending on which psychological quiz you wish to take, there are certain personality types that each of us can be categorized by. I use the basic four: Amiable, Expressive, Analytical, and Driver.

Today, the big one people use is Myers Briggs, in which there are 16 different personality types. Many companies use it today, and people often identify their personality type on dating apps to help determine compatibility with other people. It's extremely effective and accurate, far more than anyone gives it credit for. Myers Briggs, however, requires a deep understanding of psychology that is beyond the scope of this book and probably far too deep for the level of connection you're after. Honestly, even if you just observe the person as best as you can, and match everything you see and hear, you're several steps above everyone else and well on your way to building a connection.

Once I've figured out their personality, I mimic it. And then when we start talking, I agree with almost everything they say, especially when they expect me not to.

For example, if a client prefers a certain political candidate, then so do I! If their back hurts, my back hurts even more! If they live on a farm, I'll sit on a stool and start milking their cows. I don't care what their opinion is, I will make them believe it's the greatest opinion in the world. I've even met with prospects and told them THEY should be realtors... even though I'm there trying to become THEIR realtor. How crazy is that?

And it works. Here's proof.

Example #1: The Bubble Bath

I recall interviewing with a client who sat across from me, legs folded defensively, and told me he didn't want to buy a home because he sensed we were in a real estate bubble. He was expecting me to tell him, "No, there's no bubble, it'll be okay." Instead I threw him a curve ball and *agreed* with him and asked him why he felt that way! He just wanted to be heard, so I let him speak, listened intently, shut my mouth, asked intelligent questions, and agreed with him.

And because I heard him out, he heard ME out. Any other realtor would've gotten defensive, told him there's no bubble, and made statements or cited studies that showed he was wrong. Instead, I matched his bubble theory by agreeing with it. My bubble agreed with his bubble. We had a bubble bath.

The result? I put him in a home for $1.2 million. His goals and my passion, combined with my willingness to let him be heard, earned me his business. *We connected over bubbles.* Notice how my negotiating skills or track record never once factored into his decision to hire me. He simply hired me because he trusted me, and he trusted me because he liked me, and he liked me because he connected with me. Over bubbles.

Example #2: Million Dollar Calves

Did you ever think anatomy would be a reason someone would buy a house?

I had worked hard to secure a $5 million listing in the luxury market, and was hosting an open house when a man walked in with the world's shortest shorts. At first, I was a little alarmed, because with a listing that expensive, most people walking through were well dressed professionals on their best behavior. This man was dressed like he just stepped off the tennis court, and it was obvious from the size of his legs that he spent a lot of time in the gym. It threw me for a loop, momentarily scrambling my brain as I searched for a way to relate and connect with this guy.

Suddenly he rushed towards me, almost in an

aggressive manner. Bingo, I had it.

"Stop!" I said with a shocked look on my face, my arm sticking straight out in front of me with my hand up like Diana Ross and the Supremes.

He stopped dead in his tracks, unsure what I was going to say. He really didn't expect what I was about to do.

"How in the WORLD do you get your calves looking like that!?" I asked.

I then bent over, grabbed the bottom of my pants, and rolled them up. I've always been notorious for my calves, since they're almost nonexistent.

"Look at this!" I continued. "I'm 47, I work out like a beast, and I have NO calves! What's your secret?"

"Oh these?" he answered. "Ah it's nothing, I just train really hard."

Here were two grown men, in a $5 million luxury home, bending over and showing each other their calf muscles. I was admiring his while he was feeling sorry for mine.

We bonded over calves.

By the end of the day, he had referred me to a $2.5 million buyer. All because we loved each other's calves.

Example #3: Cat Scratch Fever

My wife and I are extremely allergic to cats. So, imagine my dismay when I interviewed with a prospective client who was a cat lady. Her entire home was filled with her prized cat, along with all the fur that dropped from it.

When I showed up to deliver my presentation, any other agent in my position would've asked to do it elsewhere. Maybe the car? The coffee shop down the street? Maybe she could come over to my home office?

Nope. I put my *life on the line* and went to her house.

Not only did I enter that house with my custom suit, ready to track all kinds of hair and pet dander, I also picked up that cat, held it close, and smothered my face in it. I had her convinced that I LOVED her cat, and by the time I left her house, she was convinced I was going to adopt it.

Did I survive? Hardly. *I damn near suffocated.*

But I told myself that if I don't bury my face in her cat's belly, she would hire another agent. I can guarantee you no other realtor she interviewed even paid attention to her cat, let alone risked his own life by inhaling about three hairballs down his throat like I did.

Needless to say, I got the listing.

Reject Rejection

You will get rejections all the time, whether it's real estate or any other profession. Even in relationships, there are countless times you'll get rejected.

On its own merits, rejection is difficult. We take it personally, and there isn't a human being alive who likes the feeling of being rejected. It hurts, it sucks, and it can cause you to become so jaded that even a handful of them can cause you to switch careers, give up, or not approach someone who may end up one day being the love of your life.

The key to *rejecting rejection* is realizing that everyone goes through it. You're not immune to feeling like nobody wants you. When you see someone who seems to have it all, it's imperative you know that person got to where he/she is by being told No tons of times.

Rejection is cool! Borrowing from the previous chapter, flip the switch. Be grateful for the opportunity to be heard, and use rejection as a tool for learning what you did wrong so that you can improve upon it. No one is rejecting you personally. They are rejecting the representation of you. All you have to do is change that, and your rejection rate will dramatically dwindle next time.

Embrace rejection; become numb to it. What matters isn't that you got rejected, but how you process it and respond to it. Do you hide in a corner and play the victim, crying your way out of it? Or do you thank the person for the opportunity, go back to the drawing boards, figure out what you did wrong, and come back with a vengeance?

I experienced a subtle form of rejection when my neighbors to my right, left, and front all hoisted up For Sale signs in front of their homes. They all *knew* I was a real estate agent, yet they still never hired me. I took it personally, and probably shouldn't have. Maybe they knew a friend or family member who was agent, and thus that's why they didn't hire me? Either way, it wasn't a good feeling.

Rather than give them all the silent treatment, I waited for one of their listings to expire. I then called him up, gave him my presentation, and sold his house.

This business, like any business, is hard. Yet that's also why it's so great! If it was easy, then everybody would be excelling at it, and I wouldn't have this opportunity.

One of my mentors used to tell me that whenever I failed to step up to the challenge, that I didn't want it bad enough. That really hit a nerve with me. Because we all know that if we want something bad enough, we'll find a way to make it happen. Whether it's that pair of shoes or new car or fancy new phone, we'll find a way to get our hands on it.

For me, I want to grow old with my wife. I want to watch my children grow up, get married, and have their own children. I want to serve my clients at a high level so they can have an amazing experience and tell everybody they know. These things are too damn important to me to NOT want them bad enough.

It's only through courage that I overcame my learning disabilities and turned my weaknesses into strengths by applying the principles I've outlined for you here. It all begins with passion, and having the courage to pick up the phone and call people and ask for their business. I don't spend any money on marketing. My business is driven by the telephone. I call my loved ones and friends and say, "Hi, it's Albert Garibaldi, and I'm thinking about you."

Do you understand how powerful that is? People rarely use the phone anymore for talking. So, when you do, it means that much more. I call future clients, present clients, and even past clients. This is a referral driven business. Yours is too, whatever your job is. There are always better opportunities out there, and you can only get them by reaching out to everyone you know. And that takes courage. So does passion.

Your 5-Step "Courage" Plan

To summarize, passion and courage are in-herently ineffective without the other. Cour-age is not a trait you need to spend money or time learning; it's already within you. Here's how to get it:

First, **get uncomfortable** by leaving your comfort zone in the dust. Pick a task or skill related to your goals that completely fright-ens you, and once you feel that fear in the pit of your stomach, you know you've aban-doned your comfort zone.

Next, **prepare yourself** for the challenge ahead. Do your homework, research, prac-tice, get acquainted with the environment, and make yourself numb to the thought of doing whatever it is you're about to do.

Third, **bring a friend or mentor** on your jour-ney with you. This may take a while, but will save you immeasurable time in the long run by cutting your learning curve down to a frac-tion of what it otherwise would be. A friend will support you, while a mentor will teach you. Find one, or both, and get to it.

Next, use this newfound courage to **connect**

with people. Become an award-winning connector. Determine their personality style, and match it to win them over. Get them to connect with you by getting them to **trust** you. And get them to trust you by getting them to **like** you. Read the anecdotes I gave to see examples of this in motion.

Finally, learn to **reject rejection**. Understand that everyone goes through it, and that the most successful people are the ones who *got rejected the most*.

Fail to acquire courage, and you will shortchange yourself of the life you so badly want and deserve. Passion is not enough. Gain the courage to overcome your weaknesses, and you'll be one step closer to your passion PUNCH to success!

CHAPTER 5

H is for Happiness

Happiness is the result of passion.

I'm so happy, my *face hurts.*

What is Happiness?

Passion may be what drives us; that's why I wrote a whole book on it and continue giving speeches about it. But is it the end goal?

No.

The end goal, of course, is to be happy. Happiness is the reason we do almost everything we do, even if we don't realize it. We don't want success for the sake of being successful, we want success because we think it will make us happy. We don't want to fall in love so that we can fight with our partner and nag each other all day, we fall in love because we think it will make us happy. We buy things we think they will make us happy. We hang out with friends and go to social events because we think they'll make us happy.

Whether those things make us happy or not, the point is that we do them because we THINK they will.

Happiness is the **ultimate goal**.

There would be no point to finding our passion, or to waking up in the morning and living life in general, if happiness weren't the ultimate goal. Everything we do should be towards attaining 100% leisure, and thus, 100% happiness. *All roads lead to happiness.*

If you're not living life with the goal of being happy, then you're not living life. You were blessed with the gift of life, and you owe it to yourself to make it a good one. Why would you want anything else? To be miserable? Well if misery makes you happy, then go for it. But for me, what makes me happy are the three top priorities I've stated numerous times in this book:

1. My health and fitness
2. My family and friends
3. My career

What does happiness feel like? I'm fairly certain you've felt it before, even if you're not currently happy with where you are in life. We've all had those moments where we smile so big that it hurts, that make us feel good, and where nothing can bring us down.

Perhaps someone threw you a birthday party once, and all your friends and family were there. Maybe it was your wedding day, where you were the center of attention and someone thought you were so special that he/she pledged to spend the rest of his/her life with you. Or it was the day you graduated high school or college, achieving a diploma that represented years of hard work. Or maybe it's as simple as the day you and your partner went on your first date, and you knew you had found someone you really liked.

Whatever the occasion, you knew happiness as soon as you felt it. Your goal is to capture that feeling, stuff it in a bottle, and carry it around with you wherever you go.

How to Find Ultimate Happiness

When I won the Intero Value Award in 2009, someone said about me, "I've known Albert for 12 years, and have never ONCE seen him in a bad mood."

How do you know when you've achieved ultimate happiness? When someone says that same exact thing about YOU.

I learned happiness from my father. The one thing everyone always noted about him was that he never seemed to be in a bad mood. He had his challenging moments, of course, just like we all do. But he was very careful about never letting anyone see them and not letting his negative emotions control him. When he entered a room, his loud, enthusiastic voice would echo throughout the room. His very presence alone made you feel good, that's how infectious his happiness was. I grew up watching him, observing how good he made people feel, and taught myself to do the same thing no matter what kind of mood I might be in.

The first step to finding ultimate happiness is to be honest with yourself and **take a happiness audit**. Very simply, are you happy with your life right now?

Be 100% honest. It's okay to not be in a bad mood sometimes; that's normal and even necessary. For the most part, however, do you wake up with energy, excited to take on the day? Are you passionate about what you do? Are you passionate about the relationships you have with your family, friends, and loved ones?

Now take out a pen and make a list. Write down everything in your life that you're happy about, and everything that you're NOT happy about. Make this list your guiding light. Aim to focus more time and energy on the things that make you happy, and just as much energy and time (if not more) on fixing the things that aren't.

The next step is to **find your passion**.

While it sounds like I'm stating the obvious, it really is critical you evaluate your passion as part of your happiness audit.

Some of you may have already found your passion, and that's great. For those of you who haven't, this is crunch time! This is the whole theme of this book, so take the time to really explore and find the things that make you passionate.

Write down everything you think about and talk about the most. Chances are, you'll see a pattern of things that consume your thoughts. What do you think and talk about that makes your eyes light up? If you could do any of those things for a living, would you consider it 'work?' Does it give you enthusiasm every time you think about it or talk about it?

If you can't make a living with your passion, can you at least make it a big part of your life so that it brings you more happiness?

If you answered No to any of those questions, you haven't found your passion yet. Continue to explore, discover new things, and try different activities. Exit your comfort zone if necessary. Learn to never say No to invitations or offers to go somewhere or do something. You never know what you might experience and enjoy. This is how you find opportunities. This is how I found real estate.

You want to find something that dominates your thoughts and lights a fire under your belly.

It needn't be a cliché hobby like singing, dancing, or playing music. Those things are fine, and if any of those are your passion, go for it! Don't limit yourself, however. Your passion might be as simple as doing yoga, fixing cars, helping people through medicine, decorating your home, practicing mixed martial arts, or baking cakes. Whatever it is, make sure it checks all the boxes and makes you want to get up in the morning.

Also, don't limit yourself to just one passion! Happiness and passion aren't just about your career, but also other aspects of your life. Your health, your kids, your spouse, your pets, your house, your money… there's no limit to what you can do with this gift of life you've been given.

Next, **eliminate assholes from your life**. Negative people, thoughts, and emotions will weigh you down and prevent happiness from entering your life. Even if you do experience something happy, a negative element can quickly take it away. Eliminate the negativity, and I promise you will be much happier almost instantly.

This may be a painful exercise. You're going to have to write certain people out of your life whom you may have known a very long time. Maybe some of them are family members. Perhaps some are coworkers who are inescapable.

That's okay. If you can't eliminate certain people outright, then do your best to limit your exposure to them. Do not contact them as often. Minimize your dealings with them, and as your mood begins to improve, they will notice it. They might even try to bring you down so you can be negative like they are (negativity loves company). DO NOT LET THEM! The key is to identify negative people and eliminate or minimize them enough to where they won't affect your good mood.

Eliminate or reduce other negative elements from your life. Maybe watching too much news or spending too much time on social media makes you feel angry, anxious, or negative. If so, don't do those things anymore, or cut back on them. Maybe your partner is an anchor, bringing you down. Or your job. Take an audit, make a list, and work on reducing your exposure to negativity in your life. Make the changes NOW. Your results will be almost instant.

Now to do the opposite, **seek out positivity**. If you eliminate all the negative people from your life, that's great, but you'll quickly find yourself feeling lonely. When that happens, you'll go back to those people and old habits and patterns. To avoid this trap, you must ACTIVELY seek out positivity.

Find people who are happy in life, or at least who are trying to work on it, and befriend them. Replace the dark clouds you just banished with rays of sunshine who will make you feel good about yourself. You want people who encourage and support you, not constantly knock you down just to make themselves feel better. If they're in a good mood, you will be too.

Do more of the activities that make you happy. If you used to watch the news every night, try to swap it with a comedy or motivational video. You will become what you focus on. Play music that makes you feel good, or exercise instead of heading for the sofa. Invite friends over who put you in a good mood, or talk to them on the phone. Laugh. Smile. Be positive!

We're almost done. Now that you've identified the positivity and negativity in your life, and you're working to enhance one and diminish the other, it's time to **focus on gratitude**.

Gratitude is funny. It's actually quite easy to be grateful for what we have, from our loved ones to our home, to even basic things like the ability to breathe and taste good food or smell the roses outside.

The tricky part about gratitude is that we'll be thankful for something we have, and then forget about it. We'll attend someone's funeral and be grateful for our lives... for about an hour. Then we'll go back to our everyday lives and forget about it, ready to bitch and complain about the next minor nuisance that comes our way.

Do NOT fall into this pattern. Learn to be grateful ALL THE TIME. Every time your kid drives you crazy, be grateful you have a child in the first place. Whenever you have a bad day at work, be thankful you're employed and not standing on the street corner looking for work like so many others.

How can you do this? By making it part of your daily routine. Make gratitude as automatic as brushing your teeth or taking a shower. Once you make it a daily ritual for a few weeks, it will become automatic and you won't even have to think about it anymore. It will become a part of you, and once that happens, gratitude will be automatic.

Your 5-Step "Happiness" Plan

Remember, happiness is your ultimate goal. There should be no other reason for you to exist than to obtain sustained happiness with your life.

Happiness is a state of mind, and there are realistic steps you can take to get there, starting today. Let's summarize:

First up, **take a happiness audit**. Take the time make a list, with two columns, and write down everything that makes you happy, and everything that doesn't. Focus on doing the things that make you happy, and spend just as much time fixing everything that doesn't. It won't be long before your happiness column grows in length, and you'll start seeing a major difference in your mood and your life. People you haven't seen in years will wonder what happened to you! Your old self and mood will be almost unrecognizable.

Next, **find your passion**. Happiness is the ultimate goal and result from finding your true passion, which means passion leads directly to your permanent good mood. Get proactive in exploring and doing new things, and try as much as you can until you find something that *dominates* your thoughts and makes you come alive when you think and talk about it. Learn to say Yes to invitations and offers from friends so that you experience activities that are outside your comfort zone. If you haven't found your passion yet, you never know when it will come and where it will come from.

Eliminate assholes from your life. You can follow every other step on this list, and it will be fruitless unless you complete this step. Negative emotions and people are anchors that will work hard to bring you down to their level. Your true friends will want you to succeed, while people who revel in your failure were never your friends to begin with. Eliminate (or dramatically reduce) your exposure to negativity in your life. This may require making a list, however the benefits from this painful exercise will be almost immediate.

Seek out positivity! Now that most of the negativity is gone, it's absolutely critical you replace it with positive people and emotions or else you'll feel lonely and quickly go back to your old ways. Do NOT ignore this step; it's crucial! A life absent of negativity is still a lonely, empty life unless it's quickly replaced by positivity. Find people who are happy and positive, and befriend them and spend time with them. Find activities that make you feel good, and do them more often. Your mood will quickly change and you will love it and attract more positivity like a snowball.

Finally, **focus on gratitude**. Be thankful for even the most simple and basic things in life, from the moment you wake up. To make this automatic, make it part of your daily ritual. After a few weeks, you will no longer have to think about it and it will become part of your very being. By focusing on gratitude, you will put yourself in a constant state of happiness that makes it very difficult to stray from. Write down everything you're grateful for, and look at that list every day. Make the list grow. There's no limit to what you should be grateful for in this life you've been gifted.

Follow these 5 steps and you'll be well on your way to finding happiness in your Passion PUNCH to success!

CHAPTER 6

The Passion PUNCH to Success

Bringing it all together

Passion is not enough.

You heard me. Reading this book, hearing me speak, and memorizing the P, U, N, C, and H are all great, but they're not enough to make a difference in your life.

What matters now, with all the knowledge you've acquired within these pages, is that you **take action**. How many times have you been to a motivational speech, gotten inspired to change your life, and then forgotten about it the next day? That's exactly what I DON'T want to happen to you here.

It's easy for me to talk about my passion, however the challenging part for me in writing this book was conveying to you HOW to implement these principles. I don't want you to close this book and stick it on your bookshelf for years, only to donate it to the used bookstore the next time you clean out your house. I want to create an actionable, step by step, how-to plan for you to start NOW and stick to it.

For this reason, I will summarize the key points and concepts for you here. After that is a 14-day action plan for you to follow, so that you'll have it all laid out for you and know exactly what to do next.

P = PATIENCE

Without patience, success simply isn't feasible. Rome wasn't built in a day, and neither will your dream life.

I constantly stress about the important of staying fit and healthy in order to give yourself the energy to enjoy all the other priorities in your life. What good is a great life if it won't last very long and you're not healthy enough to enjoy it? Getting in shape and feeling strong takes time, so to give yourself the patience it takes to stick with it, make sure to:

- **Hold yourself accountable**. Tell all your friends and family about your new exercise program and healthy way of eating. That way if you ever slack off, everyone will know. Share your progress and don't let anyone down, most importantly yourself. I post regular pictures on social media, which motivates myself and my followers, and holds me accountable.

- **Join something**. Get a personal trainer, join an exercise class, buy a DVD program, or do whatever it takes to give yourself a structured plan to aid you in your efforts. I have a personal trainer and she motivates me to get up early every morning.

- **Switch up your routines**. This prevents boredom and jumpstarts growth because you don't want your body to get used to the same exercises over and over again.

- **Bring a friend**. Exercising with a friend or neighbor provides support and motivation to keep going, and also makes it more fun.

When it comes to relationships, patience is the backbone that gets you through the rough times.

- **WANT it to last**. It takes not one of you, but both of you to really want the relationship to last. If one of you is committed and the other isn't, then find someone who is willing to be. The desire to make it last must be present for everything else to work.

- **Communicate, commit, and have passion**. Problems between the two of you are far more easily addressed when you can openly talk about them. Commit to communicating and making it work, and ask yourself if you have the same passion for your partner that you did when you first met.

- **Almost everything is workable**. There is no problem before you that hasn't already been experienced by another couple. Seek help, see a counselor, do your research, ask questions, or join support groups to get answers that can help whatever it is you're going through.

- **Don't rush**. If you're not in a relationship, take your time and be patient in finding someone who meets all of the qualifications above.

Be patient in your career, and use every minute of the day to advance yourself while you wait.

- **Find a mentor**. This can't be stressed enough, and there's zero chance I'd have succeeded without a strong mentor guiding me every step of the way early on. Take the time to find someone willing and capable to burst through that learning curve.
- **Leverage momentum**. Everything becomes easier after you jump the first major hurdle. If you make one sale, for example, use that momentum to make three more sales instead of basking in your own glory.
- **Lead with passion**. Focus on your passion and the money will follow. Lead with money and nothing will follow.

It takes time to **brand yourself**, but the good news is that if you lack experience or a certain skill set, **passion trumps everything**. Whether you're applying for a new job or trying to win someone's business, you can overcome almost anything by displaying genuine passion. I've scored real estate listings on my excitement level alone.

Build relationships! While extremely time consuming, this is perhaps the most important tool you can utilize. Spend the majority of your time building solid relationships. I promise they will pay themselves forward for years to come. When the real estate market crashed in 2006 and 2007, rather than cry at my desk, I built relationships with banks and secured an exclusive REO account with a major bank that netted me hundreds of home sales.

Remember, patience is NOT a waste of time. Passion and patience are both free, so use them judiciously!

U = UNSTOPPABLE

When I nearly lost my home in 2001 when the tech bubble crashed, I damn near panicked. Then I became unstoppable and never looked back. Here's how you can do the same.

Give yourself **energy**! Adapt a **caveman mentality**, where you enter **survival mode**. Tell yourself that failure isn't an option, because it really isn't. **Feed your body** with the right foods, hydrate yourself, get enough sleep, and find something that makes you passionate. Do all of these things, and you will not have a problem recruiting the energy you need to power through anything.

Show **enthusiasm**. This is the fun part! And it's automatic; once you have energy and passion taken care of, getting excited is easy because it doesn't have to be manufactured. If you're not excited and enthusiastic about what you're doing, keep looking for another passion because you haven't found it yet.

This is the only life you're ever going to live. Make it count by dressing for success and becoming unstoppable. Once you have that, success is effortless and feeds upon itself.

Give off positive vibes and energy, and the rest will take care of itself.

N = NO EXCUSES

Excuses will block you from achieving what you want, and unfortunately, it's very easy for your brain to come up with them. Here's how to re-train your brain to abolish excuses once and for all:

- **Flip the switch**. This should be your automatic response to negative triggers in your brain. Immediately turn excuses on their heads when you find yourself making them. Ask yourself why you SHOULD do something instead of why you shouldn't. Ask the right questions, and your brain will find the answers.
- **Expect** problems to happen. Nobody lives a picture-perfect life, and if they say they are, they're lying. By expecting challenges as part of your **new normal**, you'll be prepared to deal with them.
- **Embrace** your problems. When something goes wrong, train yourself to get

excited! It's an opportunity to learn, grow, solve them, and reduce the chances they'll happen again.

C = COURAGE

Perhaps the most important element of the PUNCH is courage. I learned this at a young age, when I was diagnosed with learning disabilities that would've otherwise held me back had I not had the courage to face my fears head on.

Courage isn't easy to get, but anyone can do it. We all have it within us, and here's how to draw it out of you:

- **Get uncomfortable**. By stepping out of your comfort zone, you're forced to grow as a person. If you're not continually trying new things that terrify you, then you're still living in your comfort zone.
- **Prepare yourself**. Whatever it is you're planning to do, get acclimated by practicing, researching, learning the new environment, and preparing yourself as much as possible before diving in.

- **Bring a friend and/or mentor**. Friends make uncomfortable activities more comfortable *without* sacrificing growth. They also make it more fun. Mentors teach you tricks of the trade you can't learn in books, and their help will be invaluable to you.

Once you have courage, you can better **connect** with people. The #1 trait people value in someone they know is trust, and you gain trust through likability. And you become likeable by connecting with people. Learn to become an award-winning connector. Identify someone's personality type and try to mimic it and get them to like you. Remember my stories about the bubble bath, the million-dollar calves, and cat scratch fever as funny inspirations.

Reject rejection. Flip the switch and embrace rejection as an opportunity to prove someone wrong and try harder. Become numb to rejection, because the most successful people in life were all heavily rejected (and still are).

H = HAPPINESS

Happiness is the ultimate goal in life, whatever your path or passion is. The end goal is always the same: to be happy. Here's how to find it:

- **Take a happiness audit**. Are you happy right now? Take note of everything in your life that makes you happy, and everything that doesn't. Focus equally on both, to make your lives happier AND work on fixing what's not.

- **Find your passion**. If you haven't found it yet, go forth and look. What do you get excited thinking and talking about? If you could do it as your career, would it seem like work? Explore, discover, try new things, and don't stop until you find something that dominates your thoughts.

- **Eliminate assholes**. Negativity is a heavy anchor that will weigh you down. Eliminate or reduce negative people and forces in your life, and you will experience more happiness almost immediately.

- **Seek out positivity**. Eliminating negativity without replacing it with something new will simply push you back to the dark side. Replace what you got rid of with positive people, activities, and thoughts. You must actively do it; it won't happen on its own.

- **Focus on gratitude**. Be grateful all the time by making it a daily part of your routine. Wake up and think about what you're thankful for, and after a few weeks of this, it will be automatic. We need to constantly remind ourselves what we're happy and grateful for, or else we'll get sucked into the daily cycle of life and forget about it. And once you lose something you're grateful for, you may never get another second chance. Live a life of gratitude instead a life of regret.

I challenge you. Discover your passion. Exude patience. Become unstoppable. Offer no excuses. Exercise courage, challenge yourself. Commit to happiness. Live life as though it matters.

This is the **Passion PUNCH** to success. You can do this!

Bonus: 14-Day Passion PUNCH to Success Regimen

Day 1

ELIMINATE A**HOLES from your life. This is by far the easiest step you can take to see immediate results! Take a good look at your life, and take note of all the negative forces, including toxic people, wasteful tasks that put you in a bad mood, and everything else you do throughout the course of your day. It may take courage to remove some of these things from your life, and they will do their best to suck you back in (negativity and misery love company). Resist this temptation and ignore the feelings of guilt. Do not get caught up in the vacuum of negativity that can easily suck you in. Your life will change instantly, and you'll wish you had taken this vital step much earlier.

Day 2

REPLACE THE A**HOLES in your life. Now that you've eliminated the negativity from your life, it's equally important that you immediately replace it with some positive forces. If you don't, you will feel lonely and fall right back into the sea of negative emotions you just escaped from. Seek out and befriend positive, passionate people. Do more of the things that make you happy, and fewer of the things that don't. Take up fresh, new hobbies, or further engage yourself in those you already do that bring you happiness. Whatever you do, don't be alone and don't just sit there wondering what to do with all this new free time you will have. Out with the old, in with the new!

Day 3

LIST YOUR TOP 3 PRIORITIES. These will become the new focus of your life, because the more you think about them, the more you'll work towards them and nurture them. For me, it's my health and fitness first, so that I can better serve my family and friends second, and my career and clients third. Your priorities may match mine, or they may be different. That's ok, what matters is that you identify them and make them the central focus of your life.

Day 4

CONDUCT A HAPPINESS AUDIT. Make a list of everything in your life that makes you happy, and another list of everything that doesn't. Spend an equal amount of time doing more of the things that bring you happiness, and fixing or eliminating all the things that don't. The purpose of this exercise is to give you laser like focus so that you take action on specific things instead of wandering aimlessly trying to figure it out. Only by writing them down and constantly updating your list will you begin to see real, positive results.

Day 5

FIND YOUR PASSION. Now that you've taken the happiness audit, you should have a good idea of the things you do every day that make you happy. You may have already found your passion in life, and if so, that's great. If you haven't, or if you're unsure, take the time today to commit to finding it. Get out there, explore, try new things, meet new people, and do not stop until you've found something that dominates your thoughts, gives you enthusiasm, and makes your eyes light up with excitement. Ask yourself that if you did your passion as your career, would it seem like work?

Day 6

CREATE ENERGY AND ENTHUSIASM. You now know what you're passionate about, so it's time to get excited! Give yourself the energy by adapting a caveman mentality, entering survival mode, and feeding your body with healthy nutrients, restful sleep, and invigorating exercise. Get enthusiastic by spending more time on your passion, immersing yourself in it, and learning new ways to make it part of your life and career. This day should be fun for you, and if it isn't, go back to Day 5 and make sure you've found your true passion.

Day 7

MIX IT UP. The purpose of today is to bring some variety into your life. Getting stuck doing the same thing over and over again is a surefire way to boredom. And when you're bored, you'll stop. It's okay to have a routine, just make sure you incorporate new things into that routine. Change up your workouts, do a new activity related to your passion, and meet new people to help you grow. Take a different route to the grocery store, or better yet, walk or bike there (if possible). Just do something different today, and feel the difference it will make in your daily life.

Day 8

FLIP THE SWITCH. Your brain will think of excuses today to not do something you should do; it happens to all of us. Pick just one excuse, and flip the switch. Instead of thinking why you shouldn't do something, think of all the reasons why you should. This mindset takes time to incorporate, so if you're having trouble adapting it, start small. That's why I said to just pick one excuse today. If you can handle more than one, go for it. Get into the habit, and soon it will be an automatic trigger.

Day 9

EXPECT AND EMBRACE your new normal. Things WILL go wrong today. Wake up today by telling yourself that you expect something bad to happen, and that when it does, you will embrace it. Remind yourself that this is your new reality, where imperfection is now perfect. If it's already perfect, then there's no room for growth or improvement. Expect the speed bump in the road, stand atop it, pound your chest, and holler like you're Tarzan. This is your chance to really learn, grow, and turn negatives into positives.

Day 10

FIND A MENTOR. This is one of your most important days! Do whatever it takes to find someone in your field of passion who has the knowledge and willingness to help and mentor you. It may be an expert who can Skype with you, or someone at work who can take you under his/her wing. Without mentorship, I would not have succeeded anywhere near as much as I did. Mentors can teach you things books and videos cannot, and they will drastically speed up your learning curve and extend your network. All successful people had others along the way who helped them and taught them. Today your job is to find one who is willing to help you, and strike up a relationship. Do not skip this step!

Day 11

GET UNCOMFORTABLE. By now you should have a good idea of where your comfort zone is. Today you're going to step out of it! Try a new activity related to your passion that will terrify you, and tackle it head on. Prepare yourself, practice it, and seek help or friends to help you. Just do it, whatever it is, and make sure it feels completely unnatural! Join Toastmasters, for example. Take a class on something that you've identified as a weakness of yours. Humble yourself and make it something you know you will not be good at, and challenge yourself. Trust me, whatever it is, it's not as daunting as you think it is.

Day 12

CONNECT WITH SOMEONE. Today may be challenging for you, however it's a skill you absolutely must master in order to succeed in anything. Your job today is to pick a stranger and connect with that person. It may be someone at the grocery store you strike up a conversation with, or a colleague at work you haven't spoken with much. To make it easier, find someone who looks friendly. Then get that person to like you by mirroring his/her personality, asking questions, and valuing what he/she has to say. Make the person like and trust you, and if you can do that, you've successfully connected. This is a skill that will benefit you for a lifetime

Day 13

GET REJECTED. You heard me correctly. You want to get rejected today. Why? To make yourself numb to it, and to learn to not take it personally. You are not going to succeed without first getting rejected a lot, so make it part of your daily life and learn how to reject rejection. You may have been rejected already by this point, while searching for a mentor or trying to connect with someone. If so, great! Do it again today, and you'll react to it far better than you did before. Ask someone something, and hope deep down inside that you get rejected. I know it sounds weird, but this is a very helpful exercise!

Day 14

BE GRATEFUL. Your last day! And it's an easy one. Quite simply, make a list of everything you're grateful for. And then, every single morning, refer to it until it's almost memorized and part of your daily ritual. Do this for a few weeks and it will soon become automatic. Practicing gratitude will make you feel thankful and happy for the things you do have in life, rather than feeling empty for the things you don't. This is your life, and you've only got one shot at it. Don't f*ck it up!

The Passion Punch in My Personal Life

And last but far from least, the Passion Punch played a huge role in my marriage to DeAnna. When we met at a nightclub in 1991, I was only 23 and she was just 21. From day one, we had a serious passion to build a life for ourselves and our future children. We wanted to build an idyllic life, similar to the one we each had growing up.

Even before we got married, we gathered what little money we had and put a down payment on our first home. We always set goals and worked towards them as a team. We hold each other accountable for the life we each want to have for our family.

I can't imagine my life without DeAnna and my three loves: Dominic, Nicolino, and my baby girl Daniella.

Here I am with my beautiful wife, DeAnna

Acknowledgement

I want to extend my deepest thanks, first and foremost to my parents, Al and Silvia Garibaldi. They're the ones who gave me the values, strength, and courage to be honest and strong.

I would like to thank Gino Blefari, John Thompson and Chris Stuart who together gave me my start in real estate and mentored me into who I am today.

And of course I thank my wife and kids. Without them, I have no Passion PUNCH!

My parents, Al & Silvia Garibaldi

THE END

www.PassionPunchtoSuccess.com

CPSIA information can be obtained
at www.ICGtesting.com
Printed in the USA
FSHW011900260119
55187FS